Quips & Quotes

OLDIE PUBLICATIONS

For Sara

First published in 2012
by Oldie Publications Ltd
65 Newman Street, London W1T 3EG

Copyright © Richard Ingrams, 2012

The author has asserted his moral rights

ISBN 9781901170160

A catalogue record for this book is available from the British Library

Typset in Baskerville and Utopia
Printed and bound in the UK by Butler Tanner & Dennis Ltd

RICHARD INGRAMS

Quips &
Quotes

A Journalist's Commonplace Book

Foreword

Come hither, idiot reader
And you shall have today
A pennyworth of poppycock
To pass the time away

Beachcomber

PAUL FOOT (right) and me while editing 'Parson's Pleasure' at Oxford

Introduction

What follows is a collection of quips and quotes assembled haphazardly over fifty or so years. I cannot vouch for the accuracy of all the quotations as I came across many of them in secondary sources. Anyone expecting references will be severely disappointed. Nor should readers hope to find a wide range of people quoted. My reading has been confined to a small band of favourites, reflecting my own rather limited tastes and interests.

There is more to this exercise than just making a collection of interesting or amusing remarks. Anyone who voices his opinions as I have done soon finds that most of what he wants to say about what vicars call 'the things that really matter' has already been said rather more memorably by someone in the past. It is reassuring to have our half-formed views confirmed by finer minds but, more importantly, to be given tips on how to survive, not in the form of a lengthy sermon but in one or two short sentences.

So what you have here, for what it's worth, is a short and simple tally of what I think and believe, what I like and dislike, what I find curious or funny, all written by other people.

I had never come across commonplace books until I met up with my school friend Paul Foot in Oxford in 1958. The idea, he explained, was that you kept a notebook in which you transcribed anything interesting you came across in the course of your reading. I started doing it the following year with the first of many quotes from D H Lawrence, then my favourite writer:

> *Horace is already a bit of a mellow varsity man who never quite forgot Oxford*

It was followed on the next page with this:

> *It is not familiarity that breeds contempt. It is the assumption*
> *of knowledge. Anybody who looks at the moon and says 'I*
> *know all about that poor orb' is, of course, bored by the moon*

Unlike me, Paul came from a political family and one that
was steeped in books. His grandfather Isaac was an obsessive
bibliophile with a library said to contain over 70,000 books.
His uncle Michael not only read books but wrote large
numbers of them himself. They all, I noticed, were in the habit
of underlining favourite passages in pencil, and I suppose
some of these found their way into their commonplace books.

Paul and I were interested in quotes for another reason.
We had both when schoolboys at Shrewsbury fallen under
the spell – an appropriate word – of our eccentric English
teacher Frank McEachran, nicknamed Kek, who made us
learn by heart and then recite an extraordinary collection
of what he called 'spells' – 'concentrated poetry sound or
sense', in his definition. They were snatches of prose and
poetry in a wide variety of languages, which he made us
chant in unison. The result was that I have gone through life,
as Paul and plenty of his other pupils did, with my head full
of fragments which often spring up out of the blue, bringing
laughter or occasionally consolation of a kind:

> *anyone lived in a pretty how town*
> *(with up so floating many bells down)*
> *spring summer autumn winter*
> *he sang his didn't he danced his did*
> ** * **
> *one day anyone died i guess*
> *(and no one stooped to kiss his face)*
> *busy folk buried them side by side*
> *little by little and was by was*
>
> e e cummings

All things are a-flowing,
Sage Heracleitus says;
But a tawdry cheapness
Shall outlast our days

Ezra Pound

Frank McEachran – aka Kek

To classical scholars like Paul and me, steeped in Virgil and Homer and made to translate English poetry into Latin and Greek, such language was intoxicating. Kek delighted in startling us with the strange rhymes and rhythms of Eliot and Auden:

Where the breadfruit fall
And the penguin call
And the sound is the sound of the sea

Under the bam
Under the boo
Under the bamboo tree

T S Eliot

This might happen any day;
So be careful what you say
        And do:
Be clean, be tidy, oil the lock,
Trim the garden, wind the clock;
        Remember the Two

W H Auden

Though Kek emphasised that his aim was to make boys sensitive to the music of words and the rhythm of poetry, there was a strongly subversive streak in his teaching which probably helped to nurture a satirical spirit in both of us, not forgetting another of our fellow pupils, Christopher Booker, the first editor of *Private Eye*.

Tomorrow for the young
The poets exploding like bombs

Kek used these lines from W H Auden's 'Spain', written in his revolutionary Thirties period, as his motto on the title page of his book of spells published in 1953. Then there were more spells like Ezra Pound on the First World War:

There died a myriad,
And of the best, among them,
For an old bitch gone in the teeth,
For a botched civilisation

In 1970 Kek published a second book, *More Spells*. But because I had not been made to learn these by heart they never had quite the same impact. They included one spell (again by D H Lawrence) which I had sent him:

No old world tumbles except when a young one shoves it over. And why should one howl when one's grandfather is pushed over a cliff? Goodbye, grandfather, now it's my turn

Kek commented 'Cruel, but no doubt biologically true'. Lawrence on the same theme (which obviously appealed to me as a twenty-year-old):

The danger of the young is that they will question everything out of existence so that nothing is left. But that is no reason to stop questioning. The old lies must be questioned out of existence, even at a certain loss of things worth having

---

TALKING POINT
All scoutmasters are homosexual
All tobacconists are fascists
George Orwell

George Orwell by TROG

School

If you want to know what the intelligentsia of Britain were thinking forty years ago, go to a public school common room

William Temple

Our men of the greatest genius have not been most distinguished for their acquirements at school or at the university

William Hazlitt

No schoolmaster whatsoever has existed without his having some private reserve of extreme absurdity

Walter Scott

No one knows how or where private schoolmasters die

Evelyn Waugh

It is perhaps as well that teachers can never realise how intensely aware of their personalities their charges are, because if they could they would be too terrified to move or open their mouths

W H Auden

WILLIE RUSHTON (left) and me as schoolboys, Shrewsbury School, 1952

My best friend at school was Willie Rushton. We were in the same house at Shrewsbury and we were both there because our fathers had been there before us. Willie was almost my exact contemporary, being only one day older.

He was one of those rare people who didn't appear ever to change. The torrid period of adolescence left him unscathed, making him the ideal companion for someone like me, prone to write love poetry or harbour hopes of becoming a missionary in Africa. Even as a twelve-year-old he was a brilliant cartoonist, entirely self-taught, who when left to himself would cover every available scrap of paper with doodles – mostly fat bald middle-aged men with moustaches.

It was Willie who introduced me when we were both still at school to Beachcomber (J B Morton) who later became a prime influence on *Private Eye* – partly because he was, as far as I know, the first newspaper columnist to write a column parodying the style of the newspaper he appeared in (the *Daily Express*) with spoof news items, letters to the editor, gossip paragraphs, etc.

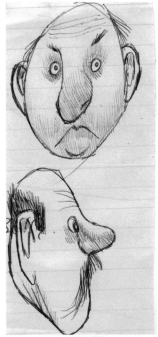

Two typical Willie doodles, found in one of my Private Eye notebooks

Beachcomber

Patience, fleas, the night is long (Spanish proverb)

Every decent man carries a pencil behind his ear to write down the price of fish

Wagner is the Puccini of music

Justice must not only be done, it must be seen to be believed

The Card Players: Willie's painting of the two of us, after Cézanne

Willie was particularly good at joke names. It was he who thought up the long-serving *Private Eye* reporter Lunchtime O'Booze. Other memorable names included Hugo Prayermat, Godfrey Hogpill, Muledamp, Voletrouser and Proudsack.

It was an art at which Beachcomber also excelled. This is his account of a society wedding headed 'Extract from the *Daily Express*':

The marriage took place yesterday at St David's, Berlin Square, of Adolf and Irene Brasch, of Boiling Springs, Crowntree, Illinois, and Iris, widow of Lt Colonel Guthrie

Tennyson and daughter of Captain and Mrs Harrison Ruck of Quetta House Aylesbury and 43 Goodwood Gardens...

In deference to the nationality of the bridegroom the couple were attended by twenty matrons of honour including Mrs Wretch, Mrs Currie, Mrs Fulkham, Mrs Dervel and Mrs Gulp. The best man was Captain 'Poodle' de Sheenie. The reception was held afterwards at Cabstanleigh House, lent by Lady Cabstanleigh for the occasion.

Those present included: Captain and Mrs Screaming, the Misses Screaming, Captain and Mrs 'Stag' Fauncewaters, Mr and Mrs Tom Watson, Lady Bumboyle, Colonel and Mrs Grundt, Lady Cabstanleigh, Miss Stultitia Cabstanleigh, Mrs Rickthorpe, Mr Prodnose, Dr Strabismus (whom God Preserve) of Utrecht, Mr Roland Milk, Master Joseph Milk, Miss Boubou Flaring, Dr Orlando Akimbo, Miss Daphne Akimbo, M. Serge Knockov, Mme Boschovskiev, Halma (the Wizard Tipsta), Miss Thake, Master Blakeney Thake, Mrs Drummond Fife, Miss Topsy Turvey, Mr and Mrs Edward Plymsolle, Miss Mimi Drake, Miss Dimity Hood, Mme Yellanda da Capo, Miss Sybil Elmcote, Dame Etiola Flaxen BBE, Dr Farribole, Mr L Gander, Lady Trasche, Mlle Fifi Barcarolle, Mrs Bradshaw and Mr Fairlie Erleigh

Like Beachcomber – at one time famous for his practical jokes – Willie was notable for his unpredictable behaviour in public. In later life he earned a lot of money as an after-dinner speaker: Barry Cryer tells the story of one such occasion when the Rotarian sitting next to him at dinner said, 'You'd better be funny tonight, Rushton, considering all the money we're paying you.' 'You're paying me that,' Willie replied, 'for having to sit next to you.'

When Willie was invited back to Shrewsbury to open a new science wing, his speech consisted of only three words: 'The bugger's open.'

His opening of a speech at an Oldie Literary Lunch:

Where would we be without a sense of humour?
(Very slight pause) *Germany!*

Another typical Willie remark, recalled by Barry Cryer, on seeing a workman bending over by the roadside:

A sitting duck for any passing deviant!

The illustration (*see right*) of one of Beachcomber's most famous sagas, 'The Case of the Twelve Red-Bearded Dwarfs', was drawn by Nicolas Bentley for a collection of Beachcomber I compiled in 1974. Bentley, the son of the inventor of the clerihew, E C Bentley, and a godson of G K Chesterton, illustrated Auberon Waugh's diary in *Private Eye* for many years, and when he died in 1978 Willie took his place. Bentley had long been an admirer of Willie's work. Reticent and quietly spoken, he was an obsessively tidy man who removed the 'h' from his name so that his two names would share the same number of letters and make his signature symmetrical.

The Case of the Twelve Red-Bearded Dwarfs by Nicolas Bentley

'Mr Justice Cocklecarrot began the hearing of a very curious case yesterday. A Mrs Tasker is accused of continually ringing the doorbell of a Mrs Renton, and then, when the door is opened, pushing a dozen red-bearded dwarfs into the hall and leaving them there'

AUBERON WAUGH by Willie Rushton

'We all have our oddities. Ingrams doesn't drink, Rushton
can't wear a tie. I would myself own up to a slight weakness
for orientals'

Auberon Waugh: *Autobiography*

Bron

Auberon Waugh, always known as Bron, was initially dubious about having Willie as an illustrator. 'Little men in black overcoats with comic moustaches and bowler hats might have appealed to the Shrewsbury set but they did nothing for me,' he wrote. But later they became inseparable, Willie providing elaborate colour cartoons for the cover of Bron's *Literary Review* as well as illustrating his Way of the World column in the *Daily Telegraph*.

Bron shared with Willie a very practical, realistic view of the world and especially the world of journalism:

Hobbit-like
I see myself as just a harmless Hobbit-like figure spreading joy and happiness and entertainment wherever I go

Stinkbottom
When I first went to boarding school at the age of six my father threatened to change my name to something like Stinkbottom. Although I knew he was only joking I never knew quite how far he was likely to take his jokes and for the first year of school life I lived in dread of every school assembly in case the headmaster suddenly announced: 'The boy you have hitherto known as Waugh will in future be called Stinkbottom'

Pipe Smokers
It is my observation that many pipe smokers are cruel, although I do not know whether their cruelty is brought on by the habit or whether cruel people are naturally drawn to pipes

True Charity
True charity requires one to chastise anything that is vile, meretricious or second-rate

I always regret never having met Bron's father, Evelyn Waugh, who died in 1966 some time before I became friends with Bron. But it was impossible to avoid his powerful spirit in his gloomy Somerset mansion, Combe Florey, to which Bron and his family moved after his death. Laura, his widow, a rather battered-looking figure, was still alive and living in a wing, and the house was filled with his Victorian furniture and paintings. It was no secret that he had died in the downstairs lavatory still decorated with two originals of two famous Charles Addams cartoons presented to him by the artist.

Evelyn Waugh

The Pagan Soul
The pagan soul has been compared to a bird flying through a lighted hall and out into the darkness. Better, to a bird fluttering about in the gloom, beating against the windows when all the time the doors are open to the air and sun

Conversation
Conversation as I love it – a fantasy growing in the telling, apt repartee, argument based on accepted postulates, spontaneous reminiscences and quotation

Possessions
By choosing preposterous objects as possessions I keep them at arm's length

The Lower Classes
It is imprudent and exorbitant to demand truth from the lower classes

The Secret of Happiness
*To make an interior act of
renunciation and to become a
stranger in the world: to watch
one's fellow countrymen, as one
used to watch foreigners, curious
of their habits, patient of their
absurdities, indifferent to their
animosities – that is the secret of
happiness in this century of the
common man*

*EVELYN WAUGH (right)
with BRON*

Marxists and Anarchists
*The disillusioned Marxist becomes a Fascist; the
disillusioned anarchist a Christian*

Painters
*Painters write well. They do most things, except choosing
clothes, better than other people: they can sail boats and
prune fruit trees and bandage cut fingers and work out sums
in their heads. The truth is that far higher gifts are needed to
paint even a bad picture than to write a good book*

Films
*There is hardly a single film for which one does not have
to make allowances. One has to make a deliberate effort to
put oneself into the state of mind to accept and enjoy the
second-rate*

Enemies of Society
*The real enemies of society are sitting snug behind
typewriters and microphones pursuing their work of
destruction amid popular applause*

The BBC
Everyone thinks ill of the BBC

Unemployed Women
*The people who keep the literary market lively are the
unemployed women, particularly in the provinces*

Failing Powers
Everyone eagerly on the watch for failing powers

The Epiphany: engraving by Eric Gill

The Epiphany
*6 Jan 1945, Communion at the Franciscan church. I had
never before realised how specially Epiphany is the feast
of artists – twelve days late, after St Joseph and the angels
and the shepherds and even the ox and the ass, the exotic
caravan arrives with its black pages and ostrich plumes,
brought there by book learning and speculation: they have
had a long journey across the desert, the splendid gifts are
travel worn and not nearly so splendid as they looked when
they were being packed up in Babylon; they have made
the most disastrous mistakes – they even asked the way of
Herod and provoked the Massacre of the Innocents – but
they get to Bethlehem in the end and the gifts are accepted,
prophetic gifts that find a way into the language of the
church in a number of places. It is a very complete allegory*

The Advance Guard
The artist, however aloof he holds himself, is always and especially the creature of the Zeitgeist: however formally antique his tastes, he is in spite of himself in the advance guard – men of affairs stumble far behind

Proust
I am reading Proust for the first time. I think he was mentally defective. I remember how small I used to feel when people talked about him and didn't dare admit that I couldn't get through him. Well I can get through him now – in English of course – because I can read anything that isn't about politics. Well the chap is plain barmy. He never tells you the age of the hero and on one page he is being taken to the WC in the Champs Elysées by his nurse and the next page he is going to a brothel. Such a lot of nonsense

Letter to John Betjeman

SEFTON DELMER playing the fool in his garden

Sefton Delmer and Claud Cockburn

The first journalist I knew was Sefton (Tom) Delmer, the chief foreign correspondent of the *Daily Express,* who had worked with my father during the War as director of the black propaganda operation. After my father died prematurely in 1953 Delmer became something of a substitute father for me and my brothers.

He lived with his second wife Peggy, a simple country girl who loved horses and who had been my father's driver in the War, in a beautiful ramshackle old farmhouse near Bures in Suffolk. There were geese and ducks in the garden, uneven brick floors, pigs in the yard and a selection of dogs and cats coming and going. Delmer, who in his youth had been a Byronic good-looker, was now an overweight shambling figure often dressed in a smock. Occasionally when sent on an assignment by the *Express* he would be transformed into an ace reporter with a dark suit, thick-rimmed glasses and a shiny briefcase. I loved him.

When I was still at Oxford I spent a summer vacation trying to teach Delmer's son, Felix, Latin. Delmer was then writing his memoirs, describing his close association with Hitler and the Nazis during the 1930s. At dinner he would read out extracts to Peggy and me, and being an arrogant young know-all, I told him that journalists were no good at writing books. By way of an answer he gave me a book called *In Time of Trouble* by Claud Cockburn.

Sefton Delmer

I can only think clearly in a five-star hotel

In real life the women pursue the men. It's only in Somerset Maugham that the men pursue the women

Poland is the Chelsea of Europe

I had never heard of Cockburn who, as his book told me, was a former columnist and correspondent of the *Times* who had published an underground one-man news sheet called *The Week* during the Thirties. Unlike Delmer's, his prose was exhilarating, his picture of the journalist's life romantic and exciting. Later, after *Private Eye* was launched and he became a regular contributor, I came to know and love him. A brilliantly clever man, he could have been a professor, but being like his friend Graham Greene a lover of mischief, and also because he had a genuine concern about all the bad things going on in the world, he chose the precarious life of a journalist.

Claud Cockburn

Bores
*One does right
to treat bores as
genuinely dangerous
characters, not
merely on account
of the debilitating
ennui with which
they enervate
one's faculties but
because there is
certainly something
dangerously wrong
with their mentality,
character and general
relationship to life*

CLAUD COCKBURN

Editors

*An editor has no business worrying himself sick about what
the public wants. He should be thinking about perfecting
and producing what he wants and then making the public
want it too*

England

The country is too small for its boots

Fires

*Whenever anything burns down, anything from the
corner shop to a warehouse, everyone's first thought is that
somebody fired it for the insurance money. It's one of the
things people know that other people do*

Facts

*To hear people talking about facts, you would think that
they lay about like pieces of gold ore in the Yukon days
waiting to be picked up – arduously, it is true, but still
definitely and visibly – by strenuous prospectors whose
subsequent problem was only to get them to market. Such
a view is evidently and dangerously naïve. There are no
such facts – or if there are, they are meaningless and entirely
ineffective until the prospector – the journalist – puts them
into relation with other facts: presents them, in other words.
Then they become as much a part of a pattern created by
him as if he were writing a novel... All this is rather difficult
and even unwholesome to explain to the layman, because
he gets the impression that you are saying that truth does
not matter and that you are publicly admitting what he
long ago suspected, that journalism is a way of 'cooking'
the facts – really cunning journalists, realising this, and
anxious to raise the status of journalism in the esteem of
the general public, positively encourage the layman in his
mistaken views. They like him to have the picture of these
nuggety facts lying about on maybe frozen ground and a*

lot of noble and utterly unprejudiced journalists with no idea whatever of what they are looking for scrabbling in the iron-bound earth and presently bringing home the pure gold of TRUTH

The above passage I was glad to see quoted with approval by another fine journalist, my friend Francis Wheen, in the introduction to his book *Hoo-Hahs and Passing Frenzies* (Atlantic, 2002).

The English
If I wrote a book about England I should call it 'What about Wednesday Week?' which is what English people say when they are making what they believe to be an urgent appointment

TALKING POINT
Cricket is nothing if it is not one man pitted against a fish
Peter Cook

Peter Cook

Grandfathers

I never met either of my grandfathers. The Reverend W S Ingrams, a master at Shrewsbury nicknamed Tush, was supposed to have got the job originally because he had a degree in botany and the Headmaster, who mistrusted science, was nevertheless required by law to appoint at least one master with a science degree (I cannot vouch for the truth of this story).

My maternal grandfather, Sir James Reid, was Queen Victoria's favourite doctor. There were pictures of him all over my granny's house in Scotland where I was brought up during the War. With his thick moustache and sideburns he looked a forbidding figure to the eyes of a little boy, but he made two very good jokes which I have always remembered.

The first was when he became engaged to the Queen's Maid of Honour, The Hon Susan Baring (my grandmother). Queen Victoria, who regarded him as her private property, was outraged, and even more outraged that he had not previously sought her permission to become engaged. Sir James apologised and assured her that it 'wouldn't happen again'.

On another occasion the staff at Balmoral were having lunch and to their surprise wine instead of the usual water was being served. Sir James asked the waiter why, to be told in a whisper, 'Prince Consort's birthday, sir.' 'I have no objection,' he replied. (It has long been a favourite expression of mine, as *Private Eye* colleagues will testify.)

SIR JAMES REID:
my maternal grandfather

Death

Death is supposed to be something we only think about in old age but I find I have quotes in my book from all stages of my life. A selection follows:

I had always supposed that the whole idea of the thing was that others might make the Obituary column but that I was immortal and would go on forever. I see now that I was mistaken and that I too must in due season hand in my dinner pail. I am not sure I like the new arrangement, but there it is
P G Wodehouse

The weak die early; and the survivors amid howling wind and plumping rain are sometimes tempted to envy them their fate

R L Stevenson

It is my experience that people who genuinely want to die soon do so

Auberon Waugh

Life is so short and death so certain, and when death comes the silence and separation are so complete, that one can never make too much of the ties and affections and relationships which bind us to the living

Violet Bonham Carter

The calm beauty of death

William Hazlitt

Curious but authenticated fact that a funeral is the only gathering to which the majority of men ever go willingly
E M Delafield, *Diary of a Provincial Lady*

If I lie down upon my bed I must be here,
But if I lie down in my grave I may be elsewhere

Stevie Smith

I cannot think of death as more than the going out of one
room into another

William Blake

At death we may have the surprise of our lives

John Stewart Collis

Dear beauteous death! The jewel of the just

Henry Vaughan

The death of great men is not always proportioned to the
lustre of their lives... The death of [Alexander] Pope was
imputed by some of his friends to a silver saucepan in
which it was his delight to heat potted lampreys

Dr Johnson

As he [Isaac Barrow] laye unravelling in the agonie of
death, the standers-by could hear him say softly, 'I have
seen the Glories of the World'

John Aubrey

Muckross Abbey by Paul Hogarth

Blessed are the dead that the rain rains upon

Edward Thomas

Sometimes death is like a fire going out gradually.
Sometimes like a gun going off, when the moment before
the explosion all is as entire as ever

James Boswell

•

Nothing else one can do but accept that weirdly convincing
promise that death isn't the end, no matter what the
evidence to the contrary
Alice Thomas Ellis (in a letter to me after the death of my daughter)

I wakened on my hot, hard bed
Upon the pillow lay my head:
Beneath the pillow I could hear
My little watch was ticking clear.
I thought the throbbing of it went
Like my continual discontent;
I thought it said in every tick;
I am so sick, so sick, so sick;
O death, come quick, come quick, come quick
Come quick, come quick, come quick, come quick

Frances Cornford

Mr Williams tells a story of some acquaintance of his
who killed himself and left a note in one of his pockets
explaining his motive to have been that he was 'Tired of
buttoning and unbuttoning'

Lord Glenbervie, *Journals*

Perhaps in Paradise we are given the power to help the living.
Sometimes I pray not for dead friends but to dead friends
asking for their help. I picture Paradise as a place of activity

Graham Greene (written ten days before his death)

And that day indeed Granny Trill died, whose bones were
too old to mend. Like a delicate pale bubble, blown a little
higher and further than the other girls of her generation, she

*had floated just long enough for us to catch sight of her, had
hovered for an instant before our eyes; and then had popped
suddenly, and disappeared for ever leaving nothing on the
air but a faint-drying image and the tiniest cloud of snuff*

Laurie Lee

*As death when we consider it closely is the true goal of our
existence, I have formed during the last few years such
close relations with this best and truest friend of mankind
that his image is not only no longer terrifying to me, but is
indeed very soothing and consoling*

Mozart (1787)

Is there life beyond the gravy?

Stevie Smith

Some obituaries

MARCHIONESS OF DUFFERIN AND AVA
*In 1980 she dismissed a butler over an issue concerning crab
apples. He took her to an industrial tribunal. Her old friend
Lord Longford offered to speak on her behalf but she assured
him 'No thank you, I am in quite enough trouble as it is'*

The Times

ELIZABETH ANSCOMBE
*Elizabeth Anscombe had a reputation for being brusque,
especially to colleagues whom she found pretentious. She
told A J Ayer, 'If you didn't talk so quickly, people wouldn't
think you were so clever.' 'If you didn't talk so slowly,' Ayer
countered, 'people wouldn't think you were so profound'*

Daily Telegraph

THE EARL OF CLANCARTY
*Brinsley Clancarty, a tall amiable figure with a rather
haunted expression and elegant braces, claimed that he could*

*trace his descent from 63,000 BC, when beings from other
planets had landed on earth in spaceships. Most humans, he
said, were descended from these aliens. 'This accounts for all
the different colour skins we've got here,' he said in 1981*
Daily Telegraph

SIR ROBERT COOKE
'Aesthetic Enthusiast in Public Life'
*Cooke was a confident personality. As one former colleague
puts it, 'He wore bold shirts and smelt of bath salts'*
The Times (sent to me by John Piper,
a connoisseur of obituaries)

W B YEATS
*I shall always remember him one morning when he stayed
with me, how he walked up and down a passage with
his hands behind his back while the house vibrated as
he hummed, his mind like a swarm of bees distilling the
golden honey of his song*
Oliver St John Gogarty

ARTHUR GASCOYNE CECIL
*British political life will be the poorer for the loss of Robert
Arthur Gascoyne Cecil, fifth Marquess of Salisbury, who
has died, aged 78. Since the Cecils made such a tremendous
intellectual comeback at the turn of the century, they have
produced scions with minds like razors, with exquisitely
sensitive souls, and with rugged opinions, the whole
encased in curiously frail-looking corporeal tenements*
Colin R Coote (Editor), Daily Telegraph

JOSEF MENGELE
*For four years after the 1939–1945 war Josef Mengele worked as
a stablehand on a farm at Rosenheim, Bavaria. The farmer was
puzzled only by the number of times his employee washed his hands*
Daily Telegraph

God

Atheists like to think they are today in the ascendancy. It may be true. But one of the difficulties facing them is the incontrovertible fact that many of the world's greatest thinkers, poets, artists and musicians have believed in God.

The Sun at His Eastern Gate by William Blake, c.1820

'What,' it will be questioned, 'when the sun rises, do you not see a round disk of fire somewhat like a Guinea?' Oh, no, no, I see an Innumerable Company of the Heavenly host, crying 'Holy, Holy, Holy, is the Lord God Almighty'

William Blake

*Once go down before the God-passion, and human
passions take their right rhythm*

D H Lawrence

*We apprehend Him in the alternate voids and fullnesses of
a cathedral: in the space that separates the salient features
of a picture: in the living geometry of a flower, a seashell, an
animal: in the pauses and intervals between the notes of
music, in their difference and sonority: and finally on the
plane of conduct, in the love and gentleness, the confidence
and humility which give beauty to the relationship between
human beings*

Aldous Huxley

*All will be judged. Master of nuance and scruple,
Pray for me and for all writers, living or dead:
    Because there are many whose works
Are in better taste than their lives; because there is no end
To the vanity of our calling: make intercession
    For the treason of all clerks.*

*Because the darkness is never so distant,
And there is never much time for the arrogant
    Spirit to flutter its wings,
Or the broken bone to rejoice, or the cruel to cry
For Him whose property is always to have mercy, the author
    And giver of all good things*

W H Auden

The one excuse for being pagan is to enjoy it thoroughly

Roy Campbell

*It is impossible to describe to people brought up on Catholic
lines of devotion what an enormous part hymns play in the
spiritual life of the ordinary not-very-religious Englishman*

Ronald Knox

The Magic Apple Tree by Samuel Palmer, c.1830

*Let us pray for each other that we may have grace to pass
through this wicked world without losing suddenly or
slowly our souls and understandings among its treacheries
and wonderfully deceiptful snares*

Samuel Palmer

If there is one thing I dislike more than theology it is geology... When Darwin, in a book that all the scientific world is in ecstasy over, proved that we are all come from shell-fish, it didn't move me to the slightest curiosity whether we are or not. I did not feel that the slightest light would be thrown on my practical life for me, by having it ever so logically made out that my first ancestor, millions of millions of ages back, had been, or even had not been, an oyster

Jane Carlyle

*There is a god in whom I do not believe
Yet to this god my love stretches,
This god whom I do not believe in is
My whole life, my life and I am his*

Stevie Smith

The riddles of God are more satisfying than the solutions of man

G K Chesterton

Catholicism is about hard facts. You know the story in St John's Gospel when he [Peter] ran to the tomb at the time of the resurrection? The beloved disciple was running behind him but he caught him up and passed him and got there first, and found the sheets piled on the left-hand side of the cave and so on. It's because it describes one disciple catching the other up and passing him that I know it must be true

Graham Greene

*I give you the end of a golden string
    Only wind it into a ball
It will lead you in at Heaven's gate
    Built in Jerusalem's wall*

William Blake

How often people speak of the absurdity of believing that life should exist by God's will on one minute part of the immense universe. There is a parallel absurdity which we are asked to believe, that God chose a tiny colony of a Roman empire in which to be born. Strangely enough two absurdities seem easier to believe than one

Graham Greene

All that is sweet, delightful and amiable in this world, in the serenity of the air, the fineness of the seasons, the joy of light, the melody of sounds, the beauty of colours, the fragrance of smells, the splendour of precious stones, is nothing but Heaven breaking through the veil of this world

Thomas Traherne

There are some feelings so complicated that though they seem indefinably, yet surely, to concern some mysterious order beyond this life, which, just as surely, we feel affects our life, they rarely find conscious expression... What if certain coincidences were really brought into being to remind us that a divine supernatural order exists? Could it be that it was rather as if, on our journey through life, some guardian spirit causes our attention to be drawn, at such moments, to certain combinations, whether of events, or persons or things, but which we recognise, as speaking to us in a secret language, to remind us that we are not altogether unwatched, and to encourage us to our highest endeavour, and especially is this true when we most need help, which is almost the same as saying when we most need assurance that our lives are not valueless

Malcolm Lowry

If you are minded thus to try, begin each day with Alfred's prayer – 'fiat voluntas tua' ['Thy will be done']; resolving that you will stand to it, and that nothing that happens in the course of the day shall displease you. Then set to any work you have in hand with the sifted and purified resolution that ambition shall not mix with it, nor love of gain, nor desire of pleasure more than is appointed for you; and that no anxiety shall touch you as to its issue, nor any impatience nor regret if it fail. Imagine that the thing is being done through you, not by you; that the good of it may never be known

John Ruskin

JOHN RUSKIN

*Whither shall I go from thy spirit?
or whither shall I flee from thy presence?
If I ascend up into heaven, thou art there:
if I make my bed in hell, behold, thou art there.
If I take the wings of the morning,
and dwell in the uttermost parts of the sea:
even there shall thy hand lead me,
and thy right hand shall hold me*

Psalm 139

Malcolm Muggeridge

When Claud Cockburn guest-edited an issue of *Private Eye* during the excitement of the Profumo Affair in 1963 he introduced me to his great friend Malcolm Muggeridge who, with his instinctive sympathy with lame ducks and black sheep, had befriended Claud when he was the editor of *Punch* – Claud then being cold-shouldered because of his Communist sympathies.

Later I formed a close friendship with Malcolm (and his wife Kitty) which was to last until his death in 1990. I owe him a great debt not only for his kindness and generosity but for shaping my view of the world, and especially the world of politics, of which he had long journalistic experience at first-hand, not only in Britain but Russia and America as well.

MALCOLM MUGGERIDGE (right) and me in his garden at Robertsbridge in 1977, when my book 'God's Apology' was published

Anthony Eden
He is not only a bore but he bores for England

Unprofitable Adulation
Nothing enrages people more than to feel they have engaged in unprofitable adulation

Lies
People believe lies not because they are plausibly presented but because they want to believe them

Power
Power, the raw material of politics, is a specialised taste: most find money and fornication and snobbishness more alluring

Men of Action
The most dangerous men of action are artists manqués

No Prejudices
Of all accounts that have been written or spoken, the ones least related to the facts are by people who affect to have no prejudices or convictions either way

Human Behaviour
Human behaviour cannot be comprehended in the concept of enlightened self-interest. Men are as liable to pursue their own ruin as their own advantage

Veneration for Power
In most people veneration for power exists quite irrespective of who exercises it

The Well-to-Do
There is nothing that gives the well-to-do greater satisfaction than to be asked to economise for the good of the country. The money saved gratifies their avarice: the fact

that in saving they are performing a public service adds a glow of self-righteousness

Myths
Public obloquy is as much a myth as public adulation: the cheers and kisses are taped, as in radio shows

An Alluring Prospect
It is always an alluring prospect to drop anything – a job, a love-affair: to creep out in the darkness from a play just before the curtain rises

As I came to know Malcolm better, I realised how much he himself had been influenced by a little-known writer and critic, Hugh Kingsmill, who had turned him from politics and journalism towards literature. Later I wrote a book about Kingsmill, Malcolm and Kingsmill's oldest friend, the biographer Hesketh Pearson. It was titled *God's Apology* after a typical Kingsmill saying: 'Friends are God's apology for relations.'

Kingsmill wrote a great many books but was never widely read, partly because he did not conform to the spirit of his times, which were serious, political and atheistic. Personally, he tended to infuriate people by being unfailingly cheerful – this in spite of his generally impoverished state.

As he himself wrote:

In their financial aspect the lives of writers, painters and musicians suggest a man leaping from ice floe to ice floe across a wide and rapid river. A strenuous, not a dignified spectacle

HUGH KINGSMILL (left) and HESKETH PEARSON

Hugh Kingsmill

Not Listening
People who can repeat what you are saying are not listening

Disciples and Friends
The last word in wisdom is not to desire disciples but to keep friends

Shyness
Shyness is egotism out of its depth

The Well-to-Do
The well-to-do do not want the poor to suffer. They wish them to be as happy as is consistent with the continued prosperity of the well-to-do

Liars and Bores
Liars are bearable if they are amusing, bores are bearable if they are accurate

Anger
To be angry is to be wrong

Vision and No Vision
Where there is no vision the people perish. I admit they also perish where there is vision. Either way, in fact, their situation appears to be damnably awkward

The Greatest Thought
The greatest thought, however far it may be from the understanding of most men, is always expressed in familiar language – 'Except a man be born again, he cannot see the Kingdom of God'

Peace
A nation is only at peace when it's at war

Systems
Systems, whatever the philosophy out of which they have grown, necessarily value truth less than victory over viral systems

The Kingdom of Heaven
Many remedies for a shattered world are now being offered to mankind but they are collective remedies, and collective remedies do not heal the ills produced by collective action. What is divine in man is elusive and impalpable and he is easily tempted to embody it in a concrete form – a church, a country, a social system or leader – so that he may realise it with less effort and serve it with more profit. Yet, as even Lincoln proved, the attempt to externalise the Kingdom of Heaven in temporal shape must end in disaster. It cannot be created by charters or constitutions nor established by auras. Those who set out for it alone will reach it together, and those who seek it in company will perish by themselves

Spiritualism
Spiritualism is the mysticism of the materialist

Snobbishness
*Snobbishness is the assertion of the will in social relations,
as lust is in the sexual. It is the desire for what divides men
and the inability to value what unites them*

A J P Taylor

Some of Malcolm's friends, like Claud Cockburn, lost touch
with him when he became a religious revivalist in his old age. An
exception was the historian A J P (Alan) Taylor, who had known
Malcolm since his days on the *Manchester Guardian* when
Taylor had been a lecturer at Manchester University. Malcolm
had wanted Taylor to speak at his funeral but as it happened
Taylor predeceased him. Alan, whom I got to know in his old
age when he was married to his third wife Eva, was, as Malcolm
often said, a loveable character despite his penny-pinching
ways. (He proudly told me once that he had calculated how
many pairs of shoes he was likely to need to see him through to
his death and had laid them down in order to save money.)

Describing himself as a 'lapsed crank', he was a typically
English combination of left-wing political opinions and
deeply conservative instincts and tastes – if not the best
certainly the most readable of modern historians.

Virtue of a Democracy
*It would be a very bad day for us when we admire our
politicians. The Germans enormously admired Hitler. And
look where it got them. The Italians thought Mussolini was
wonderful. The Russians thought Stalin was wonderful.
The great virtue of a democracy is that it always thinks its
leaders are frightful. And it's an even greater virtue of a
democracy that they always are*

A J P TAYLOR by Mark Boxer (Marc):
'He resembled a small creature of the field who was apprehensive
of attack but would turn nasty in that event' – Alan Watkins

The Jews
Years of experience have taught me that one should never venture an opinion, favourable or unfavourable, on events concerned in any way with Israel or the Jews. Any attempt at a detached view opens the way for letters, telegrams, personal expostulations and, above all, telephone calls – what the late Sir Lewis Namier called 'the terror by telephone'

Ins and Outs
I don't think our political system works except on a two-party basis: either you are for the Ins or for the Outs, there is or should be no third choice

North and South
Northern people in every country like to think of themselves as more honest and straightforward than those further south

Keeping Friends
If you once write people off because they are hypocritical or unreliable you end with no friends at all

Victims of Injustice
How much simpler life would be if the victims of injustice were attractive characters

A Single Book
The great prophets of mankind are remembered for a single book, even if they wrote many

Baring, Belloc and Chesterton

From left to right: G K CHESTERTON,
MAURICE BARING and HILAIRE BELLOC
*'I fail to see anything remarkable in what is merely a picture
of two fat men and one thin man'* – Chesterton's mother

My mother's uncle Maurice was someone I heard a lot about
when I was a boy. But I never once met him as he was an
invalid, housebound and suffering from Parkinson's. Maurice
Baring is today a largely forgotten writer, best known for
his association with two more famous figures, his friends
and fellow Catholics Hilaire Belloc and G K Chesterton. This
portrait of the three men by James Gunn used to hang in a
prominent position in the National Portrait Gallery, though
I suspect that by now it has had to give way to photographs
of the Rolling Stones and David Beckham.

Catholics like my mother – a convert like her uncle – revered all three men, but the reputation of Belloc and Chesterton has since taken a battering, mainly thanks to Belloc's ill-disguised anti-Semitism. Of the three, Chesterton has fared best. Though few of his books, apart from the famous Father Brown stories, remain in print he is one of the most frequently quoted of writers, even if he never actually said his most popular saying – that when people cease to believe in God they believe, not in nothing, but in anything. (It is worth noting that he himself once wrote: 'The act of making selections from a writer is simply the crown which awaits his fame; it is the proof of his immortality.')

BARING'S BOOKPLATE, designed for him by Hilaire Belloc.
G K Chesterton wrote of Baring:
'It is not for me to do justice here to the godlike joy of life that induced a gentleman to celebrate his fiftieth birthday in a Brighton hotel at midnight by dancing a Russian dance with inconceivable contortions and then plunging into the sea in evening dress'

Some years ago I was asked by the publisher Colin Haycraft, husband of my friend Alice Thomas Ellis, to make a collection of Chesterton quotations, but he refused to publish it because, he said, I had failed to provide any references. (Chesterton would have been amused by this, as he himself never gave a reference for any quotation and nearly always quoted from memory, frequently inaccurately.)

G K Chesterton

The Superior Man
If a man is genuinely superior to his fellows the first thing he believes in is the equality of man

Going to the Dogs
It is easy enough to say that the country is going to the dogs, if we are careful to identify the dogs with the puppies

Caricature
Caricature is a serious thing, it is almost blasphemously serious. Caricature really means making a pig more like a pig than even God made him

Hard to be Frivolous
It is so easy to be solemn; it is so hard to be frivolous... Responsibility, a heavy and cautious responsibility of speech, is the easiest thing in the world; anybody can do it. That is why so many tired, elderly and wealthy men go in for politics. They are responsible because they have not the strength of mind left to be irresponsible

Walking Behind
To walk behind anyone along a lane is a thing that, properly speaking, touches the oldest nerve of awe

AS I WOULD LIKE TO BE   *AS I AM*

Drawings by G K Chesterton

Ignorance of Youth
No man knows he is young while he is young

Dullness of the Rich
*The reason why the lives of the rich are at bottom so tame
and uneventful is simply that they can choose the events.
They are dull because they are omnipotent*

Sedentary Work
*Most of my own work is, I will not venture to say, literary,
but at least sedentary. I never do anything except walk
about and throw clubs and javelins in the garden*

A Man in Love
It is the first duty of a man in love to make a fool of himself

America
Nowhere in the world does an Englishman feel so much a stranger as in America

Madmen
Madmen are always serious – they go mad from lack of humour

Worth Doing
If a thing is worth doing it's worth doing badly

Animal Worship
Wherever there is animal worship there is human sacrifice

Neighbours and Enemies
The Bible tells us to love our neighbours and also to love our enemies, probably because they are usually the same people

Health
Of all human things the search for health is the most unhealthy

Hot Water
I believe in getting into hot water. I think it keeps you clean

Three Makes a Quarrel
It takes three to make a quarrel. There is needed a peacemaker. The full potentialities of human fury cannot be reached until a friend of both parties tactfully intervenes

A Dark Feeling
We all have a dark feeling of resistance towards people we have never met, and a profound and manly dislike of the authors we have never read

Catching a Train
The only way of catching a train I have discovered is to miss the train before

Loving the World
One must somehow find a way of loving the world without trusting it

A World Without Policemen
The young cannot imagine a world without motors. I can remember it, but I cannot imagine a world without railways. Yet I have met very old men who could remember a world without railways. Similarly, I have met very old men who could remember a world without policemen

The Pilgrim Fathers
The Americans have established a Thanksgiving Day to celebrate the fact that the Pilgrim Fathers reached America. The English might very well establish a Thanksgiving Day to celebrate the happy fact that the Pilgrim Fathers left England

Housing
It is the supreme triumph of industrial civilisation that in the huge cities which seem to have far too many houses there is a hopeless shortage of housing

A Bad Sign
It is generally a very bad sign when one is trusted very much by one's employers

E M Forster

TALKING POINT
The people I respect most behave as if they were immortal and as if society was eternal
E M Forster

Five Poems by Anon

Engraving by Thomas Bewick

The Silver Swan
The silver swan, who living had no note
When death approached unlocked her silent throat.
Leaning her breast against the reedy shore
Thus sung her first and last and sung no more;
'Farewell all joys, O death come close mine eyes
More geese than swans now live, more fools than wise'

Ernest Newman
Mr Ernest Newman*
Said 'Next week Schumann'
But when next week came
It was Wagner just the same

*A well-known music critic in his day

The Family Stein
I don't like the family Stein
There is Gert, there is Ep, there is Ein**
Gert's writings are punk
Ep's statues are junk
Nor can anyone understand Ein

Another 'Spell'
Come to our well-run desert
Where anguish arrives by cable
And the deadly sins
Can be bought in tins
With instructions on the label

Bees
Bees are bees of Paradise,
Do the work of Jesus Christ,
Do the work that no man can;
God made bees and bees make honey,
God made man and man makes money,
God made man to plough and reap and sow,
And God made little boys to scare away the crow

** Gertrude Stein, Joseph Epstein, Alfred Einstein

TALKING POINT
One half of the human race is
entertaining itself to death and the other
half is clinging to life by its fingertips
Chris Mullin

Chris Mullin by David Stoten

SAMUEL JOHNSON by Sir Joshua Reynolds, c.1775

Dr Johnson

On Opening Boswell's *Life*
*Which of us but remembers, as one of the sunny spots
in his existence, the day when he opened these airy
volumes, fascinating him by a true natural magic! It
was as if the curtains of the past were drawn aside, and
we looked mysteriously into a kindred country, where
dwelt our fathers; inexpressibly dear to us, but which
had seemed forever hidden from our eyes... Nevertheless,
wondrously given back to us, there once more it lay; all
bright, lucid, blooming; a little island of creation amid
the circumambient void. There it still lies; like a thing
stationary, imperishable, over which changeful time were
now accumulating itself in vain, and could not, any longer,
harm it, or hide it*

Thomas Carlyle

As it happens I can remember quite clearly first opening
those airy volumes – or at least one of them. It was at the
side of a swimming pool at a grand hotel somewhere in the
Loire Valley. The date must have been about 1970, and I
think the reason I remember it is because, probably under
the influence of Malcolm Muggeridge, I had taken Boswell's
Life of Johnson with me on holiday before and failed even
to open it. After that first tasting I became a Johnson addict
and have remained so ever since for reasons that are a bit
difficult to explain to the non-addict.

It was not surprising that Johnson should dominate the
thinking of somebody like Hugh Kingsmill, and to a lesser
extent Malcolm, and a great many less famous journalists,
because he was in the same line of business – writing
journalism, reviews and occasionally biographies, as in his
Lives of the Poets. Nobody has better described the nature of

such a career – its unpredictability, its pitfalls and occasional satisfactions. But Johnson does more than that. In spite of all his disadvantages – his melancholia, his ugliness, his many setbacks – he remains a very sane and sensible guide on how to cope with life, Boswell's biography in that respect being a kind of secular bible: like the Bible, a long ramshackle book with many passages of tedium but which contains buried within it some invaluable pearls of wisdom.

A Library

No place affords a more striking conviction of the vanity of human hopes than a publick library; for who can see the wall crowded on every side by mighty volumes, the works of laborious meditation, and accurate inquiry, now scarcely known but by the catalogue, and preserved only to increase the pomp of learning, without considering how many hours have been wasted in vain endeavours, how often imagination has anticipated the praises of futurity, how many statues have risen to the eye of vanity, how many ideal converts have elevated zeal, how often wit has exulted in the eternal infamy of his antagonists, and dogmatism has delighted in the gradual advances of his authority, the immutability of his decrees, and the perpetuity of his power?

The London Library

Conversation

The happiest conversation is that of which nothing is distinctly remembered but a general effect of pleasing impression

Wealth
Sir, the insolence of wealth will creep out

Sunday
Sunday should be different from another day. People may walk but not throw stones at birds

Bad Men
We form many friendships with bad men, because they have agreeable qualities, and they can be useful to us

The Blaze of Reputation
Never let criticisms operate upon your face or your mind; it is very rarely that an author is hurt by his critics. The blaze of reputation cannot be blown out but it often dies in the socket; a very few names may be considered as perpetual lamps that shine unconsumed

Ridicule and Invective
Few attacks either of ridicule or invective make much noise, but by the help of those that they provoke

Insomnia
When you cannot sleep and are beginning to think, light your candle and read. At least light your candle; a man is perhaps never so much harassed by his own mind in the light as in the dark

Truth
I said to the Doctor he might have been kinder to Gray*. He very justly said he could not be kind. He was entrusted with so much truth

People in Distress
People in distress never think that you feel enough

*Thomas Gray, the poet

Hermits
I never read of a hermit, but in imagination I kiss his feet; never of a monastery, but I could fall on my knees and kiss the pavement

Weariness
He that is himself weary will soon weary the public. Let him therefore lay down his employment, whatever it be, who can no longer exert his former activity or attention; let him not endeavour to struggle with censure, or obstinately infest the stage till a general hiss commands him to depart

Winter
To the men of study and imagination the winter is generally the chief time of labour. Gloom and silence produce composure of mind and concentration of ideas; and the privation of external pleasure naturally causes an effort to find entertainment within. This is the time in which those whom literature enables to find amusements for themselves, have more than common convictions of their own happiness. When they are condemned by the elements to retirement... they can find new subjects of inquiry, and preserve themselves from that weariness which hangs always flagging upon the vacant mind

Disease
Disease produces much selfishness... It is so very difficult for a sick man not to be a scoundrel

Kindness and Fondness
Kindness is in our power, fondness is not

Great Lords and Ladies
Great lords and ladies do not like to have their mouths stopped

Music
Had I learned the fiddle I should have done nothing else

Life
*Life to be worthy of a rational being must be always in
progression. We must always purpose to do more or better
than in time past*

Italy
*A man who has not been to Italy is always conscious of an
inferiority, from his not having seen what it is expected a
man should see*

Correspondence
*In the correspondence of your friends do not fancy that
an intermission is a decay of kindness. No man is always
in a disposition to write, nor has any man at all times
something to say*

No Man Naturally Good
*How one's heart warms to Dr Johnson when he replies to
the lady who asks him if no man is naturally good:
'No, madam, no more than a wolf'*

Graham Greene

TALKING POINT
*Why is there only one
monopolies commission?*
Screaming Lord Sutch

Screaming Lord Sutch by Robert Geary

'If that's the wife, tell her I've not been in'
Mike Williams

Drink

Drinking is a subject of great concern to a great many people, though few of them like to talk about it much. Having been advised to give it up in 1967 by a doctor friend who told me I wouldn't live much longer unless I did, I may be biased on the subject and the quotes below noted to boost my resolve. People like me will be familiar with that tempting suggestion 'But surely one glass of wine wouldn't do you any harm?' I tend to fall back on Boswell's remark about Johnson (*see right*) that I can practise 'abstinence but not temperance'.

Do you know when I see a poor devil drunk and brutal
I always feel, quite apart from any aesthetical perceptions,
a sort of shame, as if I myself had some hand in it
William Morris

Drinking makes such fools of people and people are such
fools to begin with that it's compounding a felony
Robert Benchley

I have discovered that alcohol taken in sufficient quantity
produces all the effects of drunkenness
Oscar Wilde

Nothing can be conceived more dull, more stupid, more
contrary of edification and rational amusement than
sitting, sotting over a pot and a glass, sending out smoke
from the head and articulating, at intervals, nonsense
about all sorts of things
William Cobbett

Wine makes a man better pleased with himself
Dr Johnson

Drink because you are happy, but never because you are
miserable
G K Chesterton

He could practise abstinence, but not temperance
Boswell on Johnson

I find I have been very ill all my life without knowing it. Let
me state some of the goods arising from abstaining from all
fermented liquors. First, sweet sleep; having never known
what sleep was, I slept like a baby or a ploughboy. If I wake, no
needless terror, no black views on life, but pleasing hope and
pleasing recollection. If I dream, it is not of lions and tigers

but of love and tithes. Secondly, I can take longer walks and make greater exertions without fatigue. My understanding is improved, and I comprehend Political Economy. I see better without wine and spectacles than when I use both. Only one evil ensues from it: I am in such extravagant spirits that I must lose blood, or look out for someone who will bore and depress me. Pray leave off wine – the stomach quite at rest: no heartburn, no pain, nor distension

Sydney Smith

Parties

One of the worst ordeals for the non-drinker is having to sit through a dinner party with uncongenial company. You can see why your fellow guests get drunk because it's the only way they can get through the evening. Drinks parties, as one gets older, are almost as bad because of the noise which grows louder and louder the more drink is consumed. For me one of life's greatest pleasures is slipping away, hopefully unnoticed, from such a gathering and escaping into the cool and silence of the night.

The trouble in civilised life of entertaining company, as it is called too generally without much regard to strict veracity, is so great that it cannot but be a matter of wonder that people are so fond of attempting it. It is difficult to ascertain what is the quid pro quo. If they who give such laborious parties, and who endure such toil and turmoil in the vain hope of giving them successfully, really enjoyed the parties given by others, the matter could be understood. A sense of justice would induce men and women to undergo, on behalf of others, those miseries which others had undergone on their behalf. But they all profess that going out is as great a bore as receiving; and to look at them when they are out, one cannot but believe them

Anthony Trollope

THE BRITISH CHARACTER:
Disinclination to go anywhere

Pont

*What vulgarity of mind is implied in the habit of inviting
to dinner crowds of people who are all but strangers to their
entertainers! What more hateful than to have one's house
so converted into a caravanserai! If you must feed strangers,
do it at a hotel, or hire Exeter Hall. Only the most intimate
of friends should approach the hearth*

George Gissing

*...those social summonses which call upon a man either to
be bored or to lie*

Arthur Conan Doyle, *The Adventures of Sherlock Holmes*

If there is anyone here I have not insulted, then I apologise

Johannes Brahms (leaving a party)

Politics and Power

It was the Profumo Affair of 1963 which did more than anything to colour my view of politicians. Some time during that eventful year Malcolm Muggeridge introduced me to Ludovic Kennedy, who subsequently wrote a book about the trial and death of Profumo's friend, the osteopath Stephen Ward, who was made a scapegoat by the authorities. Ludo's previous book, *Ten Rillington Place*, had already done a great deal to undermine my generation's faith in British justice and the Metropolitan Police.

I have since met a fair number of politicians and have been struck by the fact that the ones I most like and admire have been the least successful in gaining high office. Much the same point is made by Hugh Kingsmill (*see below*).

What is so interesting is the preference of the world for politicians on the make to persons genuinely interested in their welfare

Hugh Kingsmill

The best government has only to be in power long enough for everyone to wish to remove it

Lenin

Politics are a mixture of anger and deceit, and these are the mortal enemies of beauty. The instant a lady turns politician, farewell the smiles, the dimples, the roses; the graces abandon her, and age sets his seal on her front

William Cobbett

MARGARET THATCHER

I am really sorry to see my countrymen trouble themselves about politics – Houses of Commons and Houses of Lords appear to me to be fools, they seem to be something else besides human life

William Blake

To choose the victim, carefully prepare the blow, satisfy an implacable vengeance, then go to bed. There is nothing sweeter in the world

Stalin

A candidate has to render himself unfit for office in order to obtain it

Adlai Stevenson

When I went to lunch last week I was asked what it felt like to be a minister and I replied I hadn't realised how frustrated I was before I got office. I feel better, physically healthier, far less tired, on top of my form by day, even though I have very long days – I may sit in conference almost without a break from nine in the morning until six in the evening, but this doesn't tire me, it exhilarates me and I feel the better for it, whereas a morning at one's desk writing an article is nearly always exasperating and frustrating because one is always striving to improve it and one always knows it could be better than it is when one's finished it. In my life as a journalist I used to wake up after a night's sleep to find I had been pounding away at an article all night, writing, rewriting paragraphs in my sleep – I haven't so far found myself taking planning decisions in my sleep. Indeed I sleep all the more soundly for having had those decisions to take in the day, for having written 'OK' on that policy document, for having been a man of action in that sense of the word

Richard Crossman

Soon after I had received my first major architectural assignments from Hitler, I started occasionally experiencing feelings of anxiety in long tunnels, in planes or in close rooms. My heart would begin pounding, I would struggle for breath, my diaphragm would feel heavy and I had the feeling that my blood pressure was rising precipitously... The complaints vanished without medical treatment after the beginning of the war when Hitler's interest turned to other matters and I was no longer the focus of his attention, or of his affection either...

I would unhesitatingly say that fire was Hitler's proper element... Fire itself literally and directly always stirred a profound excitement in him. I recall his ordering showings in the Chancellery of the films of burning London, of the sea of flames over Warsaw, of exploding convoys, and the rapture with which he watched those films. I never saw him so worked up as toward the end of the war, when in a kind of delirium he pictured for himself and for us the destruction of New York in a hurricane of fire. He described the skyscrapers being turned into gigantic burning torches, collapsing upon one another, the glow of the exploding city illuminating the dark sky

Albert Speer

Lady Macbeth: *Thou would'st be great,*
Art not without ambition, but without
The illness should attend it

William Shakespeare, *Macbeth*

Compare David Axelrod to Barack Obama:
I think you have ambition but not that kind of
pathological drive*

*Race of a Lifetime: How Obama Won the White House
by John Heilemann and Mark Halperin (Penguin, 2010)

Politicians are not people who seek power in order to implement policies they think necessary. They are people who seek policies in order to attain power

Evelyn Waugh

Inside every revolutionary there is a policeman

Gustave Flaubert

No man has a right to pry into his neighbour's private concerns... but when he once comes forward as a candidate for public admiration, esteem, or compassion, his opinions, his principles, his motives, every aspect of his life, public or private, become the fair subject of public discussion

William Cobbett

Those who abuse liberty when they possess it would abuse power could they obtain it

Thomas Paine

What should alarm us about politicians is not that they break their promises but that they frequently keep them

Jo Grimond

What is extraordinary about tyrants as is evident in Cromwell and Napoleon, in not much smaller degrees than in Hitler, is not their intellectual development but the way in which they embody and act on behalf of some great collective passion. Their power resides less in their faculties than in their fitness to act as mediums

Hugh Kingsmill

No politician should ever let himself be photographed in a bathing suit

Hitler

I trust no one, not even myself

Stalin

It is generally accepted among all classes in Britain that anybody who puts himself forward to be elected as an MP must have some emotional inadequacy which requires this form of compensation

Auberon Waugh

In a dying civilisation, political prestige is the reward not of the shrewdest diagnostician but of the man with the best bedside manner

Eric Ambler

It is wonderful, sir, with how little real superiority of mind men can make an eminent figure in public life

Dr Johnson

All British political questions seem to involve fish at some stage or another

Alan Watkins

The cads have taken over

P G Wodehouse

The only way to control people is to lie to them

L Ron Hubbard

The great mass of the people will more easily fall victim to a great lie than a small one

Hitler

Government, like dress, is the badge of lost innocence; the palaces of kings are built upon the ruins of the bowers of paradise

Thomas Paine

Work

Writers, who are mostly self-employed, can take a principled view of work and overlook the fact that for most people it is a drudge. I speak as one who has always been his own boss and has seldom had to obey orders from a superior. I realise this makes me biased on the subject.

*There is no point in work
unless it absorbs you
like an absorbing game.*

*If it doesn't absorb you
if it's never any fun
don't do it*

D H Lawrence

D H LAWRENCE

After all, work is still the best way of whiling away one's life
Gustave Flaubert

*One of the symptoms of approaching nervous breakdown
is the belief that one's work is terribly important. If I were
a medical man I would prescribe a holiday to any patient
who considered his work important*
Bertrand Russell

Do you work with fear and trembling?
William Blake to Samuel Palmer

Fame, Celebrity, Success

In the Sixties, a great many very young people of whom I was one became famous overnight, and some like Willie Rushton became national celebrities thanks to television. Willie was a strong enough personality to withstand the pressures but others like Peter Cook were destroyed by them. I like to think of myself as someone who has achieved a certain amount of notoriety rather than fame.

Publicity, admiration, adulation or simply being fashionable are all worthless and are extremely harmful if one is susceptible to them

Ernest Hemingway

…that base acquiescence in success, that inexpressed and cowardly toleration of strength that exists, infamous and irremediable, at the bottom of all hearts, in all societies

Joseph Conrad

*LIBERACE:
a typical celebrity*

Celebrity is a mask that eats into the face

John Updike

A man of talent thinks more highly of himself when he has a success, a man of genius thinks more highly of the world

Hugh Kingsmill

*On every bookstall, in every magazine, you find works
telling people how to succeed. They are books showing men
how to succeed in everything: they are written by men who
cannot even succeed in writing books*

G K Chesterton

*Whatever we are intended to do, we are not intended to
succeed*

R L Stevenson

*To succeed in the world it is not sufficient to be stupid,
you must also be well-mannered*

Voltaire

Modern fame is nothing. I'd rather have an acre of land
Alfred, Lord Tennyson

*Success is the necessary misfortune of human life, but it is
only to the very unfortunate that it comes early*
Anthony Trollope

To be a failure may be one step to being a saint
G K Chesterton

Behind every successful man stands a surprised woman
Maryon Pearson
(wife of Canadian Prime Minister Lester Pearson)

*I think that failure is a more interesting condition than
success. Success changes people: it makes them something
they were not and dehumanises them in a way, whereas
failure leaves you with a more intense distillation of that
self you are*

Brian Moore

*The world is jealous of confidence and success: it loves
to detect the occasional ignorance of the omniscient, the
trivial errors of the infallible*

Hugh Trevor-Roper

JONATHAN SWIFT, bust in St Patrick's Cathedral, Dublin

*I remember when I was a little boy I felt a great fish at the
end of my line, which I drew up almost on the ground:
but it dropped in and the disappointment vexes me to
this very day, and I believe it was the type of all my future
disappointments*

Jonathan Swift

Men shut their doors against a setting sun

William Shakespeare, *Timon of Athens*

Old Age

As with everything else, there is Bad News and Good News. The Bad News is obvious to all – the failure of mental and physical faculties, loss of memory, etc. The Good News is the gradual loss of interest in advancement, in possessions and, hopefully, a heightened level of awareness of the extraordinary nature of life.

It is from the backs of the elderly gentlemen that the wings of the butterfly should burst. There is nothing that so much mystifies the young as the consistent frivolity of the old. They have discovered their indestructibility. They are in their second and clearer childhood, and there is a meaning in the merriment of their eyes. They have seen the end of the world
G K Chesterton

'Remind me – am I getting up or going to bed?'

Ray Chesterman

Nowadays we are always being told about the miseries of 'Old People', how lonely they are, how bored, how they have nothing to do, and so on – there is no end to the silly, useless lamentation on their behalf. The truth is invariably evaded. It is their own fault. An educated person is never lonely: he is never bored: he never seeks a pastime: he can never live long enough to study all the books he has not had time for in his life. These are his friends, these are his windows opening onto endless empires of interest, romance, emotion and thought
John Stewart Collis

An advantage of being older is that one hopes less and minds less

Malcolm Muggeridge

Old people have pets and mine is the USSR

Beatrice Webb

Every man desires to live long but no man would be old
Jonathan Swift

There comes a time when you no longer hope to improve things, you just try to keep them going

Auberon Waugh

*The world has fewer greater pleasures than that which two
friends enjoy in tracing back, at some distant time, those
transactions and events which they have passed together.
One of the old man's miseries is that he cannot easily find a
companion able to partake with him of the past*

Dr Johnson

*Resolutions when I come to be old:
Not to marry a young woman
Not to scorn present ways, or wits
Not to tell the same story over and over to the same people
Not to be over severe with young people, but give allowances
for their youthful follies and weaknesses
Not to talk much, nor of myself*

Jonathan Swift

*When you are old you have the advantage of looking
as though you are past it*

A J P Taylor

*An aged man is but a paltry thing,
A tattered coat upon a stick, unless
Soul clap its hands and sing, and louder sing
For every tatter in its mortal dress*

W B Yeats

*And this last blessing most,
    That the closer I move
To death, one man through his sundered hulks,
    The louder the sun blooms
And the tusked, ramshackling sea exults:
    And every wave of the way
And gale I tackle, the whole world then
    With more triumphant faith
Than ever was since the world was said
    Spins its morning of praise*   Dylan Thomas

Love, Marriage and the Sexes

The gays who invented a new word, homophobia, and called themselves gay because they didn't like the word queer, are now in the process of altering the word marriage which hitherto has described the coming together of two complementary creatures – man and woman. The forces of tradition are alas too weak to resist the change.

It may seem hard for young people to believe, but I belong to a generation and class which was told by its parents that if you wanted to sleep with a woman you would have to marry her. Along with most of my contemporaries I married in my early twenties and was a father of two before I was thirty.

If I envy anyone it is those of my friends who, unlike me, have avoided the nightmarish ordeal of divorce. But now, in my seventies, I am very happily married again – so I am not entitled to complain.

For richer for poorer doesn't mean whether you can afford TV or buy a car, but whether the person you marry grows in personality and character or falls away: and for better or worse means whether you can measure up to happiness and joy: in sickness and in health means not just cherishing someone who may get pneumonia, but someone who gets sick with longing for someone else

Daphne du Maurier

Few things irritate one more than the spectacle of a devoted wife, when one happens not to be the husband

William Gerhardi

It is astonishing how lonely a man is without his wife, how pointless everything seems

Hilaire Belloc

It is always easy to talk to someone with whom one is going to become intimate: the future casts its shadow backwards, and there is no explaining to be done, even though there is everything to explain. A stumbling, awkward first encounter rarely ripens into intimacy

Malcolm Muggeridge

The reverie of a man in love is a singular phenomenon. It consists of a small number of memories, forecasts and imaginings, repeated over and over again, till one would think the brain must weary itself beyond endurance. In some men, dreaming of this kind goes on for many hours consecutively, rendering every kind of occupation impossible

George Gissing

The same women who are ready to defend their men through thick and thin are (in their personal intercourse with the man) almost morbidly lucid about the thinness of his excuse or the thickness of his head

G K Chesterton

*There is of course no reason for the existence of the male sex
except that one sometimes needs help in moving the piano*
Rebecca West

There are days when one longs to be a woman
Gustave Flaubert

*The world is full of double beds
    And most delightful maidenheads,
Which being so, there's no excuse
    For sodomy or self-abuse*

Hilaire Belloc

*Both parents have known someone the children have never
known*

Graham Greene

*It would be mortifying to the feelings of many ladies, could
they be made to understand how little the heart of man is
affected by what is costly and new in their attire*
Jane Austen

*There are some people who state that the exterior, sex or
physique of another person is indifferent to them, that they
care only for the communion of mind with mind; but these
people need not detain us. There are some statements that
no one ever thinks of believing, however often they are made*
G K Chesterton

*A man is in general better pleased when he has a good
dinner upon his table, than when his wife talks Greek*
Dr Johnson

*There is no reciprocity. Men love women – women love
children – children love hamsters*
Alice Thomas Ellis

Children don't grow up. They disappear

Spike Milligan

When one has been married for over forty years there is something quite indestructible that grows up between people which has nothing to do with emotions in any way

George Bernard Shaw

A woman seldom runs riot after an abstraction

John Stuart Mill

Everyone I know is either married or dotty

Germaine Greer

Before any definite step can be taken in a household, there must be either complete division or loving accord between husband and wife. When their relations are indefinite it is impossible for them to make any move.

Many families continue for years in their old ruts, hated by both husband and wife, merely because there is neither complete discord nor harmony

Leo Tolstoy, *Anna Karenina*

Very marked difference between the sexes is male tendency to procrastinate doing practically everything in the world except sitting down to meals and going up to bed
E M Delafield,
Diary of a Provincial Lady

Music

Music is like an addiction, in that non-musical people are quite incapable of understanding how much it can dominate the lives of the musical. The urge to get to a piano can be quite as strong as the urge an alcoholic feels to get to a pub. Sometimes music can be very inconvenient, as when you have a symphony orchestra playing in your head and can't get it to shut up.

I realised how much I relied on music when I was doing my National Service in Korea, where there was no music, no piano, not even a decent gramophone. The withdrawal symptoms were severe.

Some of the quotes below suggest, quite rightly, that music is a moral force and one which, according to Schubert, gives us a glimpse of another more perfect world.

Great art is dignified by its humility

Robert Schumann

SCHUBERT, 1813,
by Leopold Kupelwieser

There is nothing more mysterious than a perfect chord
Claude Debussy

After hearing some music of Mozart's:
So do these lovely impressions which neither time nor circumstance can efface, remain in the mind and influence for good our whole existence. In the dark places of life they point to that clear-shining and distant future in which our whole hope lies
Franz Schubert

Bach is my best friend
Pablo Casals

*I sometimes feel that my whole life
is so ordered that I am really only
living when I sit at the piano and
there feel the creative strengths
which are still present in our too
technically orientated world*
Wilhelm Kempff

PABLO CASALS

Everything about Bruckner is humbug

Johannes Brahms

*The good musician loves being a musician: the bad
musician loves music*

G K Chesterton

*Les trois plus belles choses que Dieu ait faites, c'est la mer,
l'Hamlet et le Don Juan de Mozart*

Gustave Flaubert

If Beethoven is a prodigy of humanity, Bach is a miracle of God
Rossini

*Nothing can be more disgusting than an Oratorio. How
absurd, to see five hundred people fiddling like madmen
about Israelites in the Red Sea*

Sydney Smith

*Time may change the technique of music but can never
alter its mission*

Rachmaninov

While others mix cocktails I offer pure spring water
Sibelius

Illustration by G K Chesterton

The Abbé Liszt
Hit the piano with his fist
That was the way
He used to play

E C Bentley

Yehudi Menuhin

I was a friend and admirer of Yehudi Menuhin, who was a keen reader of *Private Eye*. He was also a keen practitioner of yoga and once sent me this picture of himself with the inscription: 'To Lord Gnome, from the Inner "I" Yehudi Menuhin (Bonham Carter), 1979.'

There is nothing like music to give a person overall co-ordination. It asks everything from the mind and the body, from the fingers to the eyes. Everything is involved and when you use everything, everything falls into place

I always hoped when I was a child that if I played well enough I would be able to make things better

When you spend your life with Mozart and Beethoven, Bach and Schumann and Brahms, you are living with great minds. It is a privilege given to very few people, for the greatest composers are those whose works convince the interpreter of the great and good truths, eternal and immutable

Useful Tips

Whales only get shot when they spout

Denis Thatcher

There might be a lot of cash in starting a new religion

George Orwell

If you wish for anything like happiness in the fifth act of life, eat and drink about one half what you could eat and drink

Sydney Smith

Never try to keep up with the Joneses. Drag them down to your level

Quentin Crisp

If it doesn't look easy we haven't worked hard enough

Fred Astaire

When all else fails, read the instructions

Anon

It is possible to put everything you want to say in a postcard

Joan Littlewood

JOAN LITTLEWOOD

Distrust all those in whom the urge to punish is strong

Goethe

The answer to mud slinging is to sling better mud back

A J P Taylor

No exit always means exit

Hugh Kingsmill

If it's old and you like it, it won't be there in the morning
Neil Simon

*There's nothing like finding something you have lost –
it gives you more pleasure than anything else*
Tony Benn

*A truly peaceful day from beginning to end is a great rarity
in this world*
Malcolm Muggeridge

A committee should consist of three men, two of whom are absent
Herbert Beerbohm Tree

*Avoid the latest fashion or you will be hopelessly out of date
in six months*
Oscar Wilde

*When something becomes the fashion, then is the time to
put a bomb under it*
Joan Littlewood

Never argue: repeat your assertions
Robert Owen

*When you burn your boats behind you what a nice blaze
it makes!*
Dylan Thomas

When you play, do not trouble who is listening
Robert Schumann

*One should not give up things because they are pleasant
(which is puritanism), but because by giving them up other
things become pleasanter*
Malcolm Muggeridge

Life is too short for second-rate hotels

Herbert Beerbohm Tree

*All quarrels ought to be avoided as nobody can possibly tell
where they will end*

Dr Johnson

*Somehow, I cannot explain why, a man ought to have
a dog. A man ought to have six legs: those other four legs
are part of him*

G K Chesterton

The best thing for being sad is to learn something

T H White

La verité n'est pas toujours bonne

Advice given to my granny by her French governess

Pour bien manger il faut bien attendre

(Another of her tips)

*A man can be told by his laughter: a bad man looks uglier,
a good one more attractive*

Leo Tolstoy

A quarrel is never about what it's about

Malcolm Muggeridge

If you can't be funny, be interesting

Harold Ross

*In human relations kindness and lies are worth a
thousand truths*

Graham Greene

Start the day with a smile and get it over with

W C Fields

It's a good thing to be laughed at. It is better than to be ignored

Harold Macmillan

Things cannot go on worse, one thinks, and then they do get worse

John Stewart Collis

Let us seek to fathom those things that are fathomable and reserve those things which are unfathomable for reverence in quietude

Goethe

I've always found that deep pessimism is an extremely good recipe for cheerfulness in life

John Mortimer

We're in a kind of pickle being human. My message seems to be let's not complain about it. Let's enjoy the pickle as best we can

John Updike

Be ye therefore wise as serpents and harmless as doves

Jesus Christ

TALKING POINT

The truly wicked often wear an air of serenity, generally associated in the popular mind with the attainment of high virtue

Alice Thomas Ellis

The serene L Ron Hubbard, founder of Scientology

Journalism

I first experienced the excitement of seeing my words in print when I was about sixteen and editor of the Shrewsbury school magazine, the *Salopian* – and I am ashamed to say that I still get a kick out of it now that I am in my seventies. The advantage of journalism as opposed to books is that you don't have to wait so long for publication. The fact that most journalism is ephemeral is no bar to one's excitement and may even be beneficial in that it stops one – or ought to – from becoming self-important.

Journalism could be described as turning your enemies into money

Craig Brown

Journalism largely consists in saying 'Lord Jones Dead' to people who never knew Lord Jones was alive

G K Chesterton

Readers have got to be annoyed

Lord Beaverbrook

It is utterly impossible to persuade an editor that he is nobody

William Hazlitt

It is my experience in twenty-two years of journalism that complaints about inaccuracy usually hide some deeper unhappiness

Auberon Waugh

What is really the matter with almost every paper is that it is much too full of things suitable to the paper

G K Chesterton

In journalism, the quicker and more urgent the better
Malcolm Muggeridge

No first-class journalist ever has a beard
John Junor

Freedom of the Press in Britain means freedom to print such of the proprietor's prejudices as the advertisers don't object to
Hannen Swaffer

Journalists are supposed to be slap-dash, academics to be cautious scholars. I do not think this distinction has any validity
A J P Taylor

It is always a bad sign in a journalist when he starts imagining that his work has any more important function than to fill up space in that day's newspaper
Auberon Waugh

The editor who writes for his own paper has a fool as a contributor
Bill Deedes

Don't believe everything you write in the newspapers
Malcolm Muggeridge

None of the legendary successes in journalism were achieved without risk – risk of offending, displeasing or incurring wrath or transgressing the law or even getting the sack. You can't have success and security in journalism
Bill Deedes

If an editor can only make people angry enough they will write half his newspaper for him for nothing
G K Chesterton

The writers of Newspapers, Pamphlets, Poems, Books, these are the effective Church of a modern country

Thomas Carlyle

Journalism always has to be experimental. A good editor goes tapping his way along, like a blind man

Malcolm Muggeridge

It is a sad fact of journalism that people only tell you your stuff is any good after you have stopped writing it

Auberon Waugh

A sinking ship is my spiritual home

Bill Deedes

TALKING POINT

There is nothing perhaps so generally consoling to a man as a well-established grievance; a feeling of having been injured, on which his mind can brood from hour to hour, allowing him to plead his own cause in his own court, within his own heart – and always to plead it successfully

Anthony Trollope

Well-established grievance: Ted Heath

William Cobbett

WILLIAM COBBETT, engraving by Francesco Bartolozzi, 1801

Whatever journalists may think, they have very little influence on the course of events. But there are one or two rare exceptions to the rule. William Cobbett (1763–1835) is one of them, one of those great Englishmen who are overlooked in the history books, being difficult, opinionated and frequently offensive. Ignored, too, in the school curriculum, despite being a master of the English language. Partly because he was so clear and so readable a writer, Cobbett was hugely influential in the campaign that resulted in the Great Reform Bill of 1832. He became a hero of mine after I read Chesterton's short book about him, and many years later I wrote one myself (published by HarperCollins in 2005).

Writing
Never write about any matter that you do not well understand

Government
It is the chief business of a government to take care that one part of the people do not cause the other part to lead miserable lives

Reviewers
...the old shuffling bribed sots called reviewers...

A Great Error
It is a great error to suppose that people are rendered stupid by remaining always in the same place

Private Life
Amongst the persons whom I have heard express a wish to see the press what they called free and at the same time extend the restraints on it with regard to persons in their private life, I have never that I know of met with one who had not some powerful motive of his own for the wish, and who did not feel that he had some vulnerable part about himself. The common observation of these persons is that 'public men are fair game'. Why public men only? Is it because their wickedness and folly affect the public? And how long has it been, I should be glad to know, since bad example in private life has been thought of no consequence to the public?

Machines
I have never liked machines, lest I should be tempted to understand them

Potatoes
For my own part, I have said before that rather than see the working people of England reduced to live upon potatoes,

*I would see them all hanged, be hanged myself, and be
satisfied to have written on my grave, 'Here lie the remains
of William Cobbett, who was hanged, because he would not
hold his tongue without complaining, while his labouring
countrymen were reduced to live upon potatoes'*

Bores
*The few times that I have ever travelled in a stage coach
I have held my tongue, and, in order to keep all quiet,
I have generally taken a French book to read*

Figures
Nothing so false as figures

Writing
*He who writes badly thinks badly, confusedness in words
can proceed from nothing but confusedness in the thoughts
that give rise to them. These things may be of trifling
importance when the actors move in private life, but when
the happiness of millions of men is at stake, they are of
importance not easily to be described*

The young William Cobbett joins the army (Cartoon by Gillray)

Silly People

I have known a handful of intellectually very clever people and have noted how prone they are to make fools of themselves. Nor are they helped by their conviction that they are right, and that the rest of us are too simple-minded to see the truth even when it is staring us in the face.

THOMAS BEWICK

Thomas Bewick was after a fashion a great man... but his method is archaic, crude and rough, and he never arrived at any great pitch in the technique of his calling... He has long since been outdistanced in his art by W J Linton, W L Thomas, Biscombe-Gardner and Roberts
Daily Telegraph, 10th January 1887

...the total integrity that marks all leaders of the legal profession
Lord Hailsham

I once asked Lady Mosley what she found so beguiling about Hitler's conversation. 'Oh, the jokes,' she said at once
A N Wilson

Don't be frightened of the Germans. Mr Hitler is a very intelligent gentleman
George Bernard Shaw

To sum up Harold Wilson is like trying to encapsulate 'War and Peace'
Marcia Williams (Lady Falkender)

What did Shakespeare do? What did he add to the world's totality? If he had never lived, things would be very much as they are. He added no idea, he altered no idea, in the growing understanding of mankind

H G Wells

On Stalin
Direct, honest-minded, no pretentiousness, no sign of wishing to be a personage, in short a businessman, completely absorbed in scientific humanism and in bringing health and happiness to all people

Stafford Cripps

What is Rome: a mother or father? It's not a city of coy architectonic curves although the roads are femininely sinuous. The palaces are beautiful but the elegance is masculine. St Peter's dome isn't the breast of a supine woman, but a great obscene testicle or the swelling in the throat of a rampant peacock

Anthony Burgess

On Bhagwan Shree Rajneesh
I came away, impressed, moved, fascinated by my experience of this man (or God, or conduit, or reminder) and the people ('be ordinary and you will become extraordinary') around him. I came away, also, to a haunting fragment of time: beside the road leading to the ashram there was, in addition to the beggars, a pedlar selling simple wooden flutes. As I passed him for the last time he was playing a familiar tune: how had he learnt it, and what he believed it to be, I could not even begin to imagine. It was 'Polly Put the Kettle On'

BHAGWAN SHREE RAJNEESH

Bernard Levin

On the engraving of Shakespeare in the First Folio:
I don't think it's the face of a man at all. I think it's the face of 'Anonymous'. Of somebody who isn't a man. Of a mask, somebody invented where there has to be somebody to conceal an identity. I can't put up with it

Enoch Powell

I first met Gore Vidal in 1947 (or was it '49?) He was very young and looked spruce and golden. He had tawny hair and eyes that made me think of bees' abdomens drenched in pollen

Stephen Spender

I know what I know what I know

Sarah Palin

TALKING POINT
The world keeps ending but new people too dumb to know it keep showing up as if the fun's just started
John Updike

John Updike

Oxford

Coming to Oxford in 1958 after two years of National Service I had little enthusiasm for academic work. In my case this meant Classics, as that was virtually the only subject I had been taught at school. What was new to me was philosophy, ancient and modern, modern consisting of asking such questions as 'What do we mean by meaning?' I was never any good at it but I think it helped me to develop a nose for nonsense of one kind or another.

In case you should think my education was wasted
  I hasten to explain
That having once been to the University of Oxford
  You can never wholly again
Believe anything that anyone says and that of course is an asset
  In a world like ours

Louis MacNeice

There is no necessary connection between liberty and democratic rule

Isaiah Berlin

Philosophy is a battle against the bewitchment of our intelligence by means of language

Ludwig Wittgenstein

Rousseau's famous remark that 'Man is born free and everywhere he is in chains' meant no more to some people than saying 'Sheep are born carnivorous and everywhere we see them eating grass'

Isaiah Berlin

*If it makes sense to speak of the mind's eye it must be
equally valid to talk of the mind's nose*
Gilbert Ryle

All the best books are wrong
P F Strawson (my philosophy tutor)

*The results of philosophy are the uncovering of one or
another piece of plain nonsense*
Ludwig Wittgenstein

*Philosophy will clip an angel's wings
Conquer all mysteries by rule and line
Empty the haunted air and gnomed mine
Unweave a rainbow*
John Keats

To be a philosopher now, one needs only to be clever
Bertrand Russell

*There are shits. There are bores. There are shit-bores.
And there are Shits of Hell.*
Maurice Bowra, Warden of Wadham College and
Vice-Chancellor of the University of Oxford
(told to me by Osbert Lancaster)

My father, an Oxford graduate, told me that this brilliantly
witty verse was found scrawled on the newly installed door
of one of the colleges. I have never seen it quoted elsewhere.

*ἄριστον μεν ὕδωρ**
I pissed on your new door
ὕδωρ μεν ἄριστον
Your new door I pissed on

*Water is best – Pindar

Three Lists

Maxims of Sir John Junor
(Editor of the *Sunday Express* 1954–1986)
An ounce of emotion is worth a ton of facts
No one ever destroyed a man by sneering
Always look forward, never back
Everybody is interested in sex and money
When in doubt, turn to the Royal Family
It is not libellous to ask a question
(from Brief Lives by Alan Watkins,
Hamish Hamilton, 1982)

*SIR JOHN
JUNOR by Trog*

The Seven Rare Things
Vision
Recovery of things past
Good cooking
Being loved
Satisfaction
Remarkable wine
Justice

Hilaire Belloc

Admiralty Stores List
Pots, Chamber, plain
Pots, Chamber, with Admiralty monogram in blue,
for hospital use
Pots, Chamber, fluted, with royal cipher in gold,
for flag officers only
Pots, Chamber, round, rubber, lunatic

England

Some years ago I was commissioned by the publishers Collins to compile an anthology about England.

After some time trying to isolate the characteristics that make English people different I realised that all I was doing was to define my own – a conviction that the country is going to pot (with overall tendency to pessimism), a devotion to home and domestic comforts, a disinclination to travel or even to accept dinner party invitations, a love of gardening, dogs, etc.

> *England: All trade dead 1.120: poverty and degradation 1.30, 2.64: fear of a civil war 2.86: Times, dismal and gloomy 2.70: see also INVASIONS*
>
> From the index of the two-volume edition of Dr Johnson's letters (1892)

'Good Lord! He can't speak English'

Pont

*There is nothing which an Englishman enjoys more than
the pleasure of sulkiness – of not being forced to hear a word
from anybody which may occasion to him the necessity of
replying. It is not so much that Mr Bull disdains to talk, as
that Mr Bull has nothing to say. His forefathers have been out
of spirits for six or seven hundred years and seeing nothing
but fog and vapour he is out of spirits too: and when there is
no selling or buying, or no business to settle, he prefers being
alone and looking at the fire*

Sydney Smith

Sound English common sense – the inherited stupidity of the race

Oscar Wilde

*Sir (said he), two men of any other nation who are shown
into a room together, at a house where they are both
visitors, will immediately find some conversation. But two
Englishmen will probably go each to a different window
and remain in obstinate silence*

James Boswell, *Life of Johnson*

Blind, tormented, unwearied, marvellous England

John Ruskin

*The English are not poetical or musical or clever – they're
very stupid and heavy – but they are for reasonable and
constitutional liberty, that a man should have his own
opinion without being knocked on the head for it*

Alfred, Lord Tennyson

No Englishman can live without something to complain of

William Hazlitt

*The English may not love music, but they absolutely love
the noise it makes*

Sir Thomas Beecham

View of St Paul's, one of the illustrations in my 'England' anthology
Engraving by John O'Connor

I can conceive of no one more objectionable than the
authentic Englishman. He is like a sheep with a sheep's
practical instinct for sniffing out its food in the field. But the
beauty of the field and the sky above is beyond his perception
Richard Wagner

Let us pause to consider the English.
Who when they pause to consider themselves they get all
reticently thrilled and tinglish,
Because every Englishman is convinced of one thing, viz:
That to be an Englishman is to belong to the most exclusive
club there is

Ogden Nash

I do not know how it is, but whenever I consider this
English society, always, beyond the human head and the
splendid torso, I find myself aware of the bestial and muck-
fouled hind-quarters

Hippolyte Taine

The English are so nice
so awfully nice
they are the nicest people in the world.

And what's more, they're very nice about being nice
about your being nice as well!
If you're not nice they soon make you feel it.

Americans and French and Germans and so on
they're all very well
but they're not _really_ nice, you know.
They're not nice in _our_ sense of the word, are they now?
D H Lawrence

Nature

The English may have the reputation abroad of being dull and prosaic but there is a strong English tradition of romance and mysticism linked to a love of nature, often amounting to a religious intensity. It is noticeable that the best known priests in the Anglican church are not saints but naturalists, men like Rev Gilbert White, Rev Francis Kilvert and Rev W Keble-Martin, who painted a famous inventory of all the country's wild flowers. When I moved to the country early in my married life I first became properly aware of nature, the weather, the pleasure of gardening, and all kinds of things that have since helped to keep me (at least reasonably) sane.

Oh, thought I! What a beautiful thing God has made winter to be, by stripping the trees, and letting us see their shapes and forms
Dorothy Wordsworth

Peter Brook

The hirundines (swallows) are a most inoffensive, harmless, entertaining, social, and useful tribe of birds; they touch no fruit in our gardens; delight, all except one species, in attaching themselves to our houses; amuse us with their migrations, songs and marvellous agility; and clear the air of gnats and other troublesome insects which would otherwise much annoy and incommode us

Gilbert White

No two days are alike, nor even two hours: neither was there ever two leaves of a tree alike since the creation of the world

John Constable

Oh what a treasure is every sand when truly understood! Who can love anything that God made too much? What a world this would be, were everything beloved as it ought to be!

Thomas Traherne

O, the unutterable darkness of the sky, and the earth below the moon! And the glorious brightness of the moon itself!

Dorothy Wordsworth

As I lay down on the grass I observed the glittering silver line on the ridge of the backs of the sheep, owing to their situation respecting the sun, which made them look beautiful, but with something of strangeness, like animals of another kind, as if belonging to a more splendid world

Dorothy Wordsworth

Of all the propensies of plants none seem more strange than their different periods of blossoming

Gilbert White

The earth without worms would soon become cold, hard-bound and void of fermentation, and consequently sterile

Gilbert White

Art thou a Worm? Image of weakness, art thou but a Worm? I see thee like an infant wrapped in the Lily's leaf

William Blake

It is not the rabbit out of the hat but the rabbit out of the rabbit that is so surprising

John Stewart Collis

To the endlessly repeated question 'When is your garden at its best?' one of the commonest replies is 'On the ninth of July'

Christopher Lloyd

CHRISTOPHER LLOYD in his Great Dixter garden

If a man cannot enjoy the return of spring, why should he be happy in a labour-saving Utopia?

George Orwell

For my part, as a thing to keep and not to sell, as a thing, the possession of which is to give me pleasure, I hesitate but a moment to prefer the plant of a fine carnation to a gold watch set with diamonds

William Cobbett

The tree which moves some to tears of joy is in the eyes of others only a green thing which stands in the way

William Blake

The Law

During my long years as *Private Eye* editor I was regularly involved with the law and lawyers, experiencing, as many people have done, feelings of frustration, acute boredom and bafflement at the way lawyers seemed to ignore all the points that I, the layman, considered important. In court it often felt as if one was involved in an Alice in Wonderland game, the rules of which were being made up as we went along.

Laws are like cobwebs, which may catch small flies, but let wasps and hornets break through
Jonathan Swift

I would not take libel proceedings if it were stated that I had killed my grandmother and eaten her
WT Stead

In a British courtroom an ordinary act like eating a sausage can be made under cross-examination to sound like some bizarre perversion
Auberon Waugh

Professional men, they have no cares;
Whatever happens, they get theirs
Ogden Nash

All professions are a conspiracy against the laity
George Bernard Shaw

It is not difficult to achieve a conviction of the innocent
Gareth Peirce

There are many pleasant fictions of the law in constant operation, but there is not one so pleasant or practically humorous as that which supposes every man to be of equal value in its impartial eye, and the benefits of all laws to be equally attainable by all men, without the smallest reference to the furniture of their pockets

Charles Dickens

There's no certainty in the law, it's a complete will-o'-the-wisp

Lord Denning

A libel case has become one of the sports of the less athletic rich – a variation on baccarat, a game of chance

G K Chesterton

The average lawyer is a nincompoop who contradicts your perfectly sound impressions on notorious points of law, involves you in litigation when your case is hopeless, compromises when your success is certain, and cannot even make your will without securing the utter defeat of your intentions if anyone takes the trouble to dispute them

George Bernard Shaw

Charles Dickens

TALKING POINT

I am quite serious when I say that I do not believe there are, on the whole earth besides, so many intensified bores as in these United States. No man can form an adequate idea of the real meaning of the word without coming here

Charles Dickens

The New Yorker

I have never been a reader of the magazine but I love the legends of the *New Yorker*'s early days, its brilliant and unlikely editor, Harold Ross, and the gang of writers and cartoonists gathered about him who made it one of the great successes of the magazine world, one which still thrives today.

Is Moby Dick the whale or the man?

Harold Ross

The sound of a telephone bell which ought to ring any minute, but doesn't, is much worse than the actual thing

Robert Benchley

ROBERT BENCHLEY, illustration by Gluyas Williams

Higgledy Piggledy, my white hen,
   She lays eggs for gentlemen.
You cannot persuade her with gun or lariat,
   To come across for the proletariat

Dorothy Parker

Nobody gives a damn about a writer or his
problems except another writer

Harold Ross

*Meanwhile, the New Yorker kept going
downhill... One evening, during that summer
of Harold Ross's greatest discontent, the
harried editor ran into Dorothy Parker
somewhere. 'I thought you were coming
into the office to write a piece last week,' he said. 'What
happened?' Mrs Parker turned upon him the eloquent
magic of her dark and lovely eyes. 'Somebody was using the
pencil,' she explained sorrowfully*

HAROLD ROSS

James Thurber

*The English language may hold a more disagreeable
combination of words than 'The doctor will see you now'.
I am willing to concede something to the phrase 'Have you
anything to say before the current is switched on?' That
may be worse for the moment, but it doesn't last long. For
continued unmitigated depression, I know nothing to equal
'The doctor will see you now'*

Robert Benchley

I know too many people

Harold Ross

*The Thames, I hear, remains as damp as ever in the face of
these observations*
   Dorothy Parker (in a review of Margot Asquith's memoirs)

*Harold Ross was a professional lunatic...
he had a profound ignorance. On one of
Mr Benchley's manuscripts he wrote in
the margin opposite 'Andromache',
'Who he?' Mr Benchley wrote back
'You keep out of this'*

Dorothy Parker

DOROTHY PARKER

All cartoonists are geniuses

John Updike

*We have in our heart of hearts not the faintest desire to see
a reader – ever. Absence is the very essence of readerhood.
Destroy that and you destroy all. Readers must remain, for
editors, a misty though rather laudable group, somewhere
out in the grey beyond – like the audience to the actor, a
dark swimming mass of half-people, honoured, respected,
distant and inviolate*

E B White

TALKING POINT
Men don't really like soup
Richard Nixon

Richard Nixon

Writers

Writers are keen, if not to justify themselves, then to try to explain, if only for their own benefit, why they do what they do. Partly because they confirm my own feeling, I find it reassuring that at least two of those quoted here claim that they write in order to have something to read.

It is observed that a corrupt society has many laws. I know not whether it is not equally true that an ignorant age has many books. When the treasures of ancient knowledge lie unexamined, and original authors are neglected and forgotten, compilers and plagiaries are encouraged, who give us again what we had before, and grow great by setting before us what our own sloth had hidden from our view
Dr Johnson

How little the all-important art of making meaning pellucid is studied now. Hardly any popular writer except myself thinks of it
Thomas Macaulay

One reason for writing, of course, is that no one's written what you want to read
Philip Larkin

To write well, lastingly well, immortally well, must not one... be prepared to endure the reproaches of men, want, and much fasting, nay martyrdom in its cause? It is such a task as scarce leaves a man time to be a good neighbour, an useful friend, nay to plant a tree, much less to save his soul
Alexander Pope

It seems to me that at least two thirds of the stuff published nowadays is by one-book people. You know, 'A Stirring

*Revelation of a Young Girl's Soul' by Jane Emmeline Banks,
who never writes another damn book in her life. The test is,
can you write three?*

P G Wodehouse

*Long books, when read, are usually over-praised because
the reader wants to convince others and himself that he has
not wasted his time*

E M Forster

*There have always been a lot of women writers.
It's something they do naturally, like sewing*

Rebecca West

*The writer should always be ready to change sides at the
drop of a hat. He speaks up for the victims, and the
victims change*

Graham Greene

On being asked why he had never written for the theatre:
*When I write a book I can devote as many hundreds or
indeed thousands of words as I like to get into my readers'
minds exactly how I want them to see my heroine. Should
I be fool enough to write a play all I can write is 'Enter
Millicent' and then I am in the hands of some damn tart
who is sleeping with the manager*

Arnold Bennett

*'The Tailor of Gloucester' – I rank it with
the masterpieces of Balzac*

A J P Taylor

*The dust and smoke and noise of modern
literature have nothing in common with
the pure, silent air of immortality*

William Hazlitt

Careers for Your Sons: Literature
The best sort of book to start with is biography. If you want to make a success of it, choose as a subject someone very famous who has had plenty of books written about him quite recently

Evelyn Waugh

A well-written Life is almost as rare as a well-spent one
Thomas Carlyle

Talking of the great difficulty of obtaining authentic information for biography, Johnson told us: 'When I was a young fellow I wanted to write the "Life of Dryden", and in order to get materials I applied to the only two persons alive who had seen him; these were old Swinney and old Cibber. Swinney's information was no more than this, "That at Will's coffee house Dryden had a particular chair for himself, which was set by the fire in winter, and was then called his winter-chair; and that it was carried out for him to the balcony in summer, and was then called his summer-chair"'

James Boswell

I don't think you can write about people if you don't feel fond of people. Ultimately you have to celebrate the human condition

William Trevor

A writer, like a priest, never retires

Graham Greene

FLASH! When the roof leaks and the piano needs tuning, when the geyser explodes... what do I do? I send for the expert, the trained man, and leave the solution of my problem to him. And when the day of reckoning comes I fix up according to the standard rates hallowed by a couple of centuries of collective bargaining. When I want to read anything, however, I usually write it meself

Flann O'Brien

Writing is a form of therapy: sometimes I wonder how all those who do not write, compose or paint can manage to escape the madness, the melancholia, the panic fear that is in the human situation

Graham Greene

Writing books, so far as the great public is concerned, is rather like throwing them into a well

Ford Madox Ford

*Cartoon by Barry Fantoni (from an idea of Peter Cook's)
The figure on the left bears a distinct resemblance
to Christopher Booker*

Edith Sitwell

Almost every booklover has a few favourite books which seem to have been overlooked by all the other booklovers. My own list includes the *Autobiography* of Edith Sitwell published in 1965, from which all the following quotes, except the first, are taken.

On Herself
The reason I am thought eccentric is that I won't be taught my job by a lot of pipsqueaks. I will not allow people to bore me. Nobody has ever been more alive than I. I am an electric eel in a pond full of flatfish

Lytton Strachey
He seemed to have been cut out of very thin cardboard

Her Mother
My father's principal worry was my mother, who had an objectionable habit of indulging in gaieties. When she died, dear old Henry Moat, my father's valet and my brothers' and my lifelong friend, said, 'Well, at least Sir George will know now where Her Ladyship spends her afternoons'

Her Father
When he was not pacing up and down the passages, my father spent much of his time walking up and down outside the house, and when he did this he would succeed in appearing like a procession of one person – he being the head, the beginning and the end

Aleister Crowley
Although Mr Crowley did his best to pursue an acquaintance with my brother and myself, I did not at the time wish to

know him. But when later on I read about the sacrifice of a wretched cat, who was not properly killed during one of the obscene rites he practised, anger made me wish I had taken the opportunity. It would have given me pleasure to have said to him: 'Mr Crowley, you will go straight to hell and you will meet only yourself, over and over again.

'Together with Lady ___ who, I hope, will talk to you.'

Lord (Gerald) Berners
A pompous woman of his acquaintance, complaining that the head-waiter of a restaurant had not shown her and her husband immediately to a table, said, 'We had to tell him who we were.' Gerald, interested, inquired, 'And who were you?'

EDITH SITWELL

Jesus Christ

Those who deny the existence of God and the divinity of Christ are still left to decide about the gospels, a piece of writing like any other. Is it fact or fiction? Does it have the 'ring of truth'? It is interesting to me how many writers, few of them orthodox Christians, have written about the gospel story and their reactions to the character of Jesus. In 1999 I published an anthology of their views *Jesus: Authors Take Sides* (HarperCollins) but it transpired that very few members of the public shared my interest in the subject.

Jesus of Nazareth sits in a chamber of every man's brain, immovable, immutable, however credited or discredited
Rebecca West

No other story, no pagan legend or philosophical anecdote or historical event does in fact affect any of us with that peculiar and even poignant impression produced on us by the word Bethlehem. The truth is that there is a quite peculiar and individual character about the hold of this story on human nature: it is not in its psychological substance at all like a mere legend on the life of a great man. It is rather as if a man had found an inner room in the very heart of his own house which he had never suspected; and seen a light from within
G K Chesterton

There's this brave, witty sometimes oddly petulant man striding around in an occupied territory knowing and then not wanting to know that he's bound to die and to die painfully. And in the middle of it all to say things that have never been said, and are still not said, about love. As a model of what human behaviour can be like, it still stands supreme
Dennis Potter

If it was proved he never existed then the invention would reflect huge credit on the human race for having had the most extraordinary idea in its history. It would take soaring genius to make him up

Alice Thomas Ellis

'And Jesus went before them, and they were amazed: and as they followed they were afraid.' Obviously that was not invented; it was a simple report of an experience of awe of a phenomenon which was amazing and which was so powerful in effect that Christianity could grow from it

John Stewart Collis

He took the entire world of the inarticulate, the voiceless world of pain, as his kingdom, and made of himself its eternal mouthpiece

Oscar Wilde

Is it any wonder that to this day this Galilean is too much for our small hearts?

H G Wells

Christ on the Cross, 'Le Dévot Christ', 1307, in the Cathédrale de Saint-Jean-Baptiste, Perpignan, France

He was so great a man that though he transmitted no writing of his own to posterity, we have his mind and his greatness handed down by others. It is to be lamented that the history of the latter was written and revised by men interested in the pious frauds of religion. Yet through all this I see his splendour

John Keats

I see the Man toiling along in the hot sun, at times in the cold wind, going long stages, tired, hungry often and footsore, drinking at the spring, eating by the way, His rough and patched clothes bedraggled and covered with dust... doing battle with that valiant voice of His, only against the proud and perverse, and charming the simple by His love and lovableness, but ever disencharming such as would suppose that the kingdom of heaven that He preached would bring to Him or to His adherents earthly glory or riches; offering them rather ignominy and death

Thomas Carlyle (speaking to Holman Hunt)

It is a great pity to allow either a bishop or an atheist to steal him away from us

Paul Potts

Christ was so infinitely great because no furniture or other silly accessories ever got in his way

Vincent van Gogh

He didn't even own a toothbrush

Henry Miller

'Now look what you've done'

Nick Hobart

Index of those quoted